G-FORCE

THE ESSENTIAL GUIDE

G-FORCE

THE ESSENTIAL GUIDE

CONTENTS

FOREWORD

Written by Jerry Bruckheimer

I've always loved adventure films, but if you can approach the genre from a different angle than what's been seen previously, the possibilities are even more exciting. That's what we tried to do with the *Pirates of the Caribbean* trilogy, combining the classic buccaneer genre with supernatural elements and lots of offbeat comedy. It's fun to take films based on familiar, even classic themes, give them a twist, and see what evolves. Movies about secret agents had been with us on screen long before James Bond blasted his way into theatres in 1962 – there's even a movie called *The Secret Agent* that dates all the way back to 1916, and twenty years after that, in 1936, Alfred Hitchcock directed Secret Agent – and they seem to be as popular now as they've ever been. And movies, either animated or live-action, in which animals speak and have personalities of their own, have also been with us for quite some time.

What we've never seen, however, is a movie about secret agents who also happen to be animals, and which is both animated *and* live-action. And what's more, in the miracle of modern, high-tech 3D!

That's what *G-Force* is. Hoyt Yeatman, our director, is an Academy Award-winning visual effects supervisor who we had already worked with on *Armageddon*. He has plenty of ideas bouncing around his incredibly fertile brain, and the one that excited him the most actually came from his son, Hoyt, Jr, who was in pre-school at the time. Out of the mouths of babes. The idea, of course, seemed utterly off-the-wall, which was just fine with us, because it was also completely original.

The amazing thing is that although little Hoyt may not have known it, the fantasy element of *G-Force* is based on certain fascinating realities. For years, the American government has engaged in top-secret programs in which they train animals to help defend the nation, from dolphins detecting mines to cockroaches carrying recording devices. Using that notion as a jumping-off point, we kick it to the next level… what if a scientist had actually figured out a way not only to train such animals, but to actually *communicate* with them? Consider the possibilities.

Guinea pigs, one of most popular household pets in western culture although originally from South America, have a DNA which is remarkably close to humans, and are (believe it or not for anyone who's had one of these meek creatures as a pet) very intelligent. So the core of G-Force are three super-cool guinea pigs: Darwin, the courageous but self-questioning squad leader; Blaster, the slightly unhinged go-getter; and Juarez, fiery but on point at all times. Joined by a brilliant mole named Speckles, who is a genius with computers, and a literal fly-on-the-wall named Mooch, G-Force is trained by a young scientist named Dr Ben Kendall to go where humans dare not – or cannot – tread.

One of Hoyt Yeatman's smartest decisions was to make the computer animated animals as photo realistic as possible instead of looking like "cartoon" critters. He won his Academy Award for his work on Disney's remake of the Willis O'Brien/Ray Harryhausen classic *Mighty Joe Young*, in which Hoyt created one of the most authentic CG animals ever to put on screen, making him a worthy successor to those special effects wizards of the past. We always push the envelope for visual effects on our films. If you saw what we did in the *Pirates* trilogy, then you know for certain that we're always going to take it a step further, and *G-Force* will take it even a step beyond that.

In *G-Force*, I don't think you'll be able to tell what was shot live and what was created in the computer by Hoyt and his amazing visual effects team, because it's the humans who bring these animals and their world fully alive. That includes the great team of actors who contribute their voices and personalities to the movie: Nicolas Cage, with whom I've had such wonderful collaborations with in the past on *The Rock*, *Con Air*, *Gone in 60 Seconds*, and the two *National Treasure* films, is the voice of Speckles; Penelope Cruz, who has given award-caliber performances in films as diverse as *All About My Mother* and *Vicky Christina Barcelona*, is Juarez; Tracy Morgan, a brilliant comedic talent from TV's Emmy-winning *30 Rock*, is Blaster; and Sam Rockwell, a really fine performer who has shined in movies like *The Hitchhiker's Guide to the Galaxy* and *Frost/Nixon*, is the stalwart Darwin. And as some of the other characters surrounding the adventure and comedy, the terrific Jon Favreau, who acted so wonderfully in *Swingers* and then showed major chops as a director with *Elf* and *Iron Man*, is Hurley, an overweight guinea pig languishing away in a pet store who finds his inner hero; and Steve Buscemi, another fantastic actor who was in *Armageddon*, is the voice of a very excitable – okay, crazy – hamster named Bucky. Add to that such live, on-camera actors as the great Bill Nighy, who so magnificently brought Davy Jones to life in *Pirates of the Caribbean: Dead Man's Chest* and *Pirates of the Caribbean: At World's End*; the very talented Will Arnett as a by-the-book FBI man; a gifted young comedian named Zach Galifianakis as Dr Ben Kendall; and the lovely Kelli Garner as Marcie, a lissome veterinarian, and you have a heavyweight group of talent lending their considerable skills to *G-Force*.

The key to *G-Force*, we hope, is that it appeals to everybody. Like the *Pirates of the Caribbean* or *National Treasure* movies, everyone in the audience, from six to sixty, can have a great time. This DK book you're holding in your hands gives you a first-class ticket right into the inner sanctum of *G-Force*, the characters, their high-tech gadgets, their bio lab, and the world in which their adventure takes place. Invisible! Invincible! Welcome to *G-Force*…

WHO IS THE G-FORCE?

It can be a crazy, mixed up world out there and we can all use a little extra-special help from time to time: We need folk who risk life and limb to save others – heroes who aren't afraid to take on bad guys, no matter how big and scary!

When times are tough, there's always room for a few more good guys and good guys don't come much better than the G-Force! Super-tough, with brains to match, the G-Force is an elite unit of highly trained secret agents, always ready to leap into action.

There's just one tiny detail you should probably know about the G-Force. They're animals. Three guinea pigs, a mole and a fly! This may seem strange, but isn't it true that some of the best things come in small packages? Maybe it's time to meet the G-Force and make up your own mind!

DARWIN

A natural born leader, Darwin has the respect of his team. In return, he trusts them with his life. He takes his role very seriously and is quick to blame himself when things don't go to plan. Under pressure, he has been known to lose confidence in his abilities. But when it really matters, determined Darwin overcomes his jitters and steps up to be the guinea pig he's meant to be.

TOUGH THINGS COME IN SMALL PACKAGES!

Pilates has made Darwin limber.

LEADERSHIP
Darwin keeps his team pulling together and focused. His upbeat outlook helps — at only 23-centimetres (9-in) tall, he sees the upside of pretty much everything!

DIGITAL DISASTER
Darwin is horrified when an extermination virus crashes his PDA. But could it be the key to bringing down a dangerous mastermind and saving the world?

Infrared scope provides good vision at night.

G-Force synchronise their watches before each mission.

Release button opens Darwin's parasail.

HANDYMAN

Whether it's taking apart a coffeemaker or firing through a plasma screen, Darwin is a good guinea pig to have around in a DIY crisis.

Fur hides a birthmark in the shape of an American Eagle.

G-FORCE GENERAL

Darwin can really pack a punch! Thanks to his grueling fitness regime, he is the peak of furry physical perfection. His shoulders may look small but they are strong enough to bear all the burdens this leader piles on himself.

DID YOU KNOW?
Guinea pigs are not pigs and are not from Guinea. They are a type of rodent that orginally came from South America.

JUAREZ

Agent Juarez has it and boy does she flaunt it! This sassy señorita's beauty is only matched by her bravery and her martial art skills. She doesn't just keep up with the boys, she beats them, saving their skin more often than not! This is one feisty furball you should never underestimate!

FEARLESS
Juarez thrives on action and adventure. Leaping off high buildings with a parasail is no challenge for her.

Acrobatics have made Juarez strong and flexible.

Juarez keeps in shape by working out on an elliptical training module.

WHAT A CUTIE!
When it's time to play cute to attract an adoptive family, Juarez has it in the bag. She's chosen by a girl called Penny. But Juarez is in for a surprise! Penny has some plans for her new pet – and they involve make-up!

FACT FILE
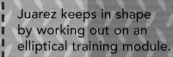
NAME: Juarez
SPECIALITIES: Security and defence
SKILLS: Martial arts
INTERESTS: 1970's funk music and grooming

Juarez knows how to use her eyes to stop villains in their tracks. She just needs to bat her eyelashes!

MASTER OF MARTIAL ARTS!

Delicate wrists are fitted with military hardware.

Although perfectly groomed, Juarez isn't afraid to get dirty on missions.

FLIRTY
This Spanish chica is no puffy pushover. She plays hard to get and likes to keep the boys guessing.

SHOCKING PINK
Tough but also feminine, Juarez has her own style and it doesn't include girly bows and ribbons! It takes a lot to make her scream, but being dressed up in pink does it! Surely that's animal cruelty?

ACTION STATIONS!
Between missions, Juarez relaxes by grooming herself or rocking it out to very loud music. But she is always ready to leap into action at a moment's notice and throw some martial art moves!

BLASTER

Agent Blaster may be small but his ego certainly isn't! This daredevil will try anything once. Blaster tears around thinking nothing of taking risks. As far as he's concerned, the more adrenalin-fueled his escapades the better! His enthusiasm is infectious and as a loyal friend and a great agent, he is an invaluable member of the crew.

RODENT SCHOLAR
As well as the brawn, Blaster also has the brains. He is a graduate of the United States Military Academy at West Point – done by correspondence of course!

Just try and stop Blaster from using this grappling hook to scale high walls!

FREEWHEELER
You'll need to watch your step when Blaster's behind the wheel! This speed junkie just loves to let loose. What's more, in a guinea-pig-sized car, there are no stop signs, no rules – just the open road!

TEAM PLAYER
Blaster knows the importance of team branding. He comes up with the group's name and invents their morale-boosting pose with fists raised high. G-Force!

DON'T MESS WITH ME!

Blaster likes to keep an eye on the ladies – especially Juarez. But that doesn't mean he understands them!

CRAZY SCHEMES

High-spirited, Blaster is famous for his loony antics. But no matter what, failure never appears to blunt his enthusiasm!

Lifting weights keeps Blaster in shape.

Blaster looks good and boy does he know it!

BRAVADO

Blaster pretends to be fearless but his friends know that underneath he's a real softie. He refuses to admit defeat and maintains he's indestructible, even when Juarez saves him from a fierce Doberman!

FACT FILE

NAME: Blaster
SPECIALITIES: Weapons and transportation
SKILLS: Ballistics
INTERESTS: High-speed driving and Juarez

Pack contains all the gadgets a guinea pig may need when he's on a mission!

SPECKLES

Agent Speckles coordinates G-Force missions from behind the scenes. Nothing happens that he doesn't know about! But life can be tough when you're a mole and poor Speckles is no exception. Tragedy, persecution and rejection are his experience of humans. Embraced by the G-Force, blind Speckles finds acceptance and friendship. But is that enough for this troubled mole?

FAMILY TRAGEDY

Speckles's underground home was destroyed and his family exterminated just to make way for a golf course! It's enough to give anyone a grudge against humanity.

BLIND AND BRILLIANT!

DINNER TIME

There's nothing Speckles likes more than munching on a nice tasty earthworm. Delicious and nutritious!

COMPUTER WHIZZ

Called ugly and limited by his sight, Speckles takes refuge in computers. His fingers dance across his customised Braille keyboard like lightning.

Moles are blind because they are designed to thrive below ground.

Special G-Force glasses help Speckles to see better.

FACT FILE

NAME: Speckles
SPECIALITY: Cyber intelligence
SKILLS: Code breaking
INTERESTS: Plotting revenge

Claws made for burrowing are also good for typing.

NO LIMITS

This star-nosed mole may be weak and have blurry vision but his IQ is off the charts. Speckles knows how to use his brain power to more than make up for any physical limitations.

UNDERESTIMATED

His G-Force comrades regard Speckles as one of them. They are sympathetic to his suffering but they don't realise the lengths he will go to for revenge.

MOOCH

Ever wished you could be a fly on the wall? Well, that's Mooch's job! Small and sneaky, he can go unnoticed by humans and slip anywhere. With his high-tech video surveillance kit, he is the eyes of the G-Force operations. The team would be lost without him!

I'M NOT HERE FOR THE SWEETS!

SWEET TOOTH
Nothing can distract Mooch from his task. Well, almost nothing. Whenever he sees sugary treats, his candy-radar kicks in and overrules his head!

FLYING MACHINE
Mooch can flap his wings around 200 times a second! He practises his flight patterns in a wind vortex. His ability to avoid predators is like a fighter plane dodging flak.

FACT FILE
NAME: Mooch
SPECIALITY: High-tech surveillance
SKILLS: Avionics and navigation
INTERESTS: Sweets

SUPER SPY

Mooch – aka Fly 2.0 – carries a nano-camera pack that is almost as big as he is! It sends live images to the rest of the G-Force, wherever they are, so they can analyse events and plan their next move.

No human is fast enough to swat Mooch.

SAY WHAT?

Mooch can't speak, so he finds other ways to get his message across, from using a keyboard to flying up and down for "yes" and from side-to-side for "no".

Like Mooch's eyes, the tiny camera has several lenses.

Large eyes give nearly 360° vision.

Mooch can cling to walls and ceilings to get the best view.

I'M A PEST!

Mooch is the fly for the job if you need a diversion. He wreaked havoc by flying up businessman Leonard Saber's nose!

BEN KENDALL

G-Force owes its existence to visionary Ben Kendall. A government scientist, Ben has a natural affinity with animals. He believes in them and wants them to believe in themselves too, so he secretly sets up an Animal Training Programme. The idea of talking animals is too crazy for Ben's bosses to take him seriously, but he puts his faith in the G-Force.

DID YOU KNOW?
Ben also trains cockroaches! Almost indestructible, they can, with Ben's help, carry micro-cameras into surveillance zones unnoticed.

MAVERICK
Unauthorized missions are the only way that Ben can prove to the FBI what G-Force are capable of. It's risky, but determined Ben figures that it's easier to ask for forgiveness than permission.

FACT FILE
NAME: Ben Kendall
ROLE: Government scientist and G-Force founder
SPECIALITY: Training animals
INTERESTS: Inventing

UNDERCOVER
Uh-oh, the exterminator turns up and gasses the G-Force! Don't worry – this is actually Ben in an exterminator's suit. It's a clever ruse to sneak the creatures out of a danger zone.

INGENIOUS

Ben's imagination and ingenuity know no bounds. A gadget freak, he just loves inventing new gizmos and pushing the bounds of technology and science.

MARCIE HOLLANDSWORTH

As G-Force's veterinarian, clever Marcie looks after the team. It's her job to make sure they are fit, healthy and happy so they can complete their missions in tip-top condition. When the FBI raids the lab, Marcie puts her job on the line to save the G-Force.

SENSE OF HUMOUR

Quick-witted Marcie fools the gullible FBI agents Carter and Trigstad long enough for G-Force to escape. She claims an empty box is full of "stealth hamsters", made invisible by a special coating!

TEAM PLAYERS

Ben trusts Marcie to keep the secrets of the G-Force. She shares his vision and they both respect the animals, not as pets, but as fellow professionals.

FACT FILE

NAME: Marcie Hollandsworth
ROLE: Veterinarian
SPECIALITY: Exotic animals
INTERESTS: Ben

GADGETS

The G-Force is great at its job. High-tech gizmos help each of them to be even better and stronger. Team founder and scientist, Dr Ben Kendall, is happiest when he's inventing cutting-edge, guinea-pig-sized gadgets for any situation.

VISOR
When you're moving fast, you need to protect those eyes. At high speed, grit can sting!

WHIRLING BOLOS
Juarez proves that size isn't everything with these whirling bolos. When Blaster gets in a tight spot, Juarez wraps them around the snout of a snarling Doberman and saves his furry hide!

HEADSET
This ear piece has a light and communication device that allows the G-Force to keep in touch with each other in the field.

NIGHT-VISION GOGGLES
These glasses allow the G-Force to see in the dark – perfect for undercover night-time espionage!

PARASAIL

Guinea pigs might not be able to fly, but they can at least fall safely with these rodent-sized parachutes. Perfect for a quick escape off high buildings.

DIVING KIT

There's no need to swim on underwater missions – these SCUBA scooters shoot Blaster and Juarez through the water!

WATCH

These standard-issue wristwatches are a constant reminder that there isn't long before Project Clusterstorm launches.

FIELD COMPUTER

Even out on missions, Speckles has his nose up against his screen. It is portable, but is still pretty cumbersome for little Speckles to carry.

GRAPPLING HOOK

Scaling Saber's mansion is easy if you throw these hooks up to the roof and then climb up a rope. Especially for Juarez, who leaves Blaster in the dust!

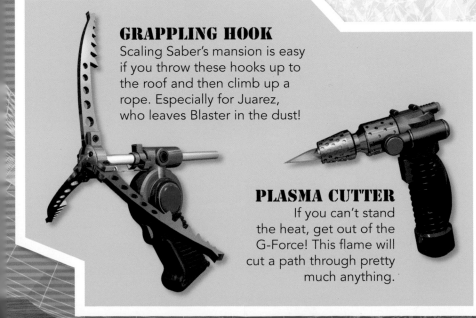

PLASMA CUTTER

If you can't stand the heat, get out of the G-Force! This flame will cut a path through pretty much anything.

USB STICK

This stores crucial data about the mysterious Project Clusterstorm.

BEN'S
WAREHOUSE

Hidden away in a dilapidated warehouse is a big surprise. Along a dark corridor, through a storeroom door is Ben's state-of-the-art biological laboratory! This is G-Force HQ – the heart of all missions and the place the animals call home. To avoid suspicion, the warehouse has a sign saying "ACME Extermination". But what happens inside is completely the opposite!

GENIUS AT WORK
The lab is Ben's favourite place to spend time. From training cockroaches to encouraging Speckles's computer superskills, it all happens here.

ORDERED CHAOS
The ramshackle lab may look a mess, but Ben knows exactly what's what and has everything he needs at his fingertips. It's the perfect secret location for a top-secret project.

WORK AND PLAY

The G-Force spends time out in the field, but they always return to the lab – their home, workplace and training ground. Juarez likes the elliptical training module. It can be hard work, but no pain, no gain!

WORK IT!

These guinea pigs are all gym bunnies. Working out keeps them healthy and in tip-top shape for their job. After all, you never know when you're going to have to outrun something bigger than you!

MOLE HOLE

Speckles's pod is darker than the others to suit his poor eyesight. Marcie keeps the humidity setting damp. For Speckles, it's the next best thing to being in a tunnel underground.

HOME SWEET HOME

Each G-Force member has their own personalised pod where they can kick back and get some privacy. Darwin's reflects his spiritual side and has colours he finds calming.

WORK IT OUT!

Saving the world can be tough on the body, so agents have to be in tip-top shape. Flexibility, stamina, speed, balance and hand-eye reflexes can all make the difference between success and facing failure. After years of research, Ben has compiled the best training guides to make furballs into fit-balls. Get set... go! Last one to finish is a gopher!

STRETCH BEFORE YOU EXERCISE
TO AVOID SERIOUS INJURY

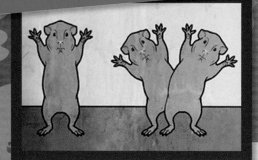

1. Lateral stretch

2. Reaching hamstring

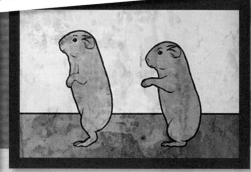

3. Hawks squat

4. Paw touch

5. Side-kick jump stretch

6. Glute hamstring stretch

DOG TARGET PRACTICE CHART
CANINE WEAKNESS POINTS

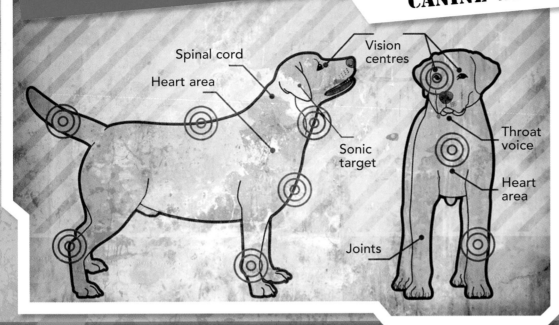

Spinal cord

Heart area

Vision centres

Sonic target

Throat voice

Heart area

Joints

Dogs may be a man's best friend, but they're no rodent's buddy. This chart helps the G-Force hone their target practice as part of their physical training programme.

WEIGHT TRAINING BUILDS STRENGTH
STRENGTH BUILDS CONFIDENCE

1. Alternating press

2. Lateral raise

3. Kneeling tricep raise

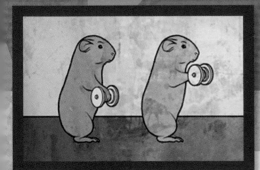

4. Reverse curl

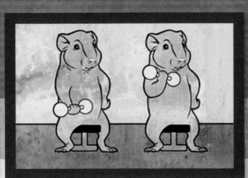

5. Concentration curl

6. Dumbbell extension

LEONARD SABER

Money makes Leonard Saber's world go round. CEO of Saber Industries, this hard-nosed business mastermind has spent his career amassing a vast fortune. Focused and ruthless, Saber lets nothing stand in his way. He has a new plan that promises to change life as we know it. But could it be that power and success have gone to his head and now he might be getting a little careless?

THE HIGH LIFE

Saber likes the finer things in life and his image matches his business mind – sharp. Well-tailored designer suits don't come cheap and his watch is worth £34,600!

FACT FILE

NAME: Leonard Saber
ROLE: Businessman
SPECIALITY: Inventor of smart appliances
INTERESTS: World domination

WORLD DOMINATION

Depite his successes, Saber never stops. His thirst for power, money and influence drives him to be the biggest and the best. He wants to change the way the whole world lives – forever.

BUSINESS MATTERS

Saber's latest venture involves a new range of domestic appliances designed for ordinary families. But all may not be quite what it seems...

HIDDEN SECRETS

The G-Force team are convinced that Saber is up to no good. Finally the FBI start listening to the animals and raid Saber's mansion. But what are they going to find?

SHOW-OFF

Leonard Saber loves the sound of his own voice. For the launch of his new smart appliances, he throws a lavish party and invites anyone who's anyone. Nothing thrills him more than playing to an audience.

CHRISTA

The young, glamourous Christa is Saber's personal assistant. At Saber Industries everything must be perfect and it's her job to make sure everything runs to Saber's exacting standards.

SABER'S MANSION

Saber switches the flames in his high-tech fireplaces on and off by clapping his hands.

LOUNGE
In his lounge Saber can relax and wow his business associates with lavish entertainment. It's a hard life being a billionnaire!

High on the hills overlooking Los Angeles sits Leonard Saber's humble home. From up here, Saber can watch over his electronics empire. A masterpiece of modern architecture, his home has been built to incorporate the latest technology and the tightest security.

Private security guards patrol the perimeter with fierce Dobermans.

STUDY

Here, Saber plots his route to world domination, undisturbed. Despite tight security, Darwin sneaks into Saber's study to download confidential information from Saber's PC.

SABERLING TECHNOLOGY

Don't miss the new Saberling 5000 series! Billionaire Leonard Saber is launching a brand new range of appliances that no household can be without! Promising to lighten the stresses of everyday life, these smart appliances combine simple design with user-friendly technology. And at the core of each product is its secret – the revolutionary SaberSense technology that will change life as we know it.

DID YOU KNOW?

Saber is working with a mysterious partner in the Far East called Mr Yanshu. He produces the appliances and the SaberSense chips.

A GLOBAL FAMILY

Leonard Saber has his eye on world domination. In every corner of the globe there are stores like this one, all selling his new Saberling 5000 series.

STACK 'EM HIGH

A retailer's dream, Saber's smart appliances are affordable and appeal to everyone. Stocked from floor to ceiling, they fly off the shelves. Even FBI Director Killian has a Saber mobile phone.

Vacuum cleaner

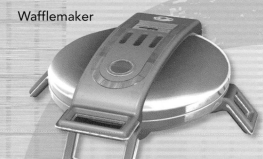

Wafflemaker

Refrigerator

Toaster

Coffeemaker

Food mixer

Blender

Washer and dryer

SABERSENSE

The secret in the heart of every Saber product is a SaberSense microchip. SaberSense is a wireless system that links all the chips inside the appliances so they can communicate with one another. This means your fridge can tell you when you're running out of food! Life will never be the same again...

FBI AGENTS

FBI stands for the Federal Bureau of Investigation. The organisation works for the United States' government to protect the country. They are the good guys who keep everyone safe.

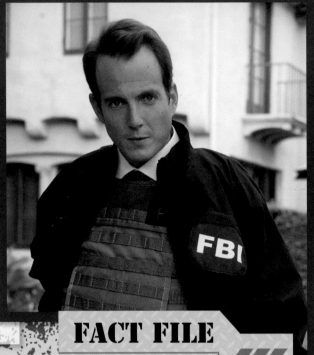

KIP KILLIAN

Recently promoted, Killian loves his new-found power. He is sometimes focused on his career, but when it really matters, he proves he's a good guy at heart.

FACT FILE

NAME: Kip Killian
ROLE: Director of an FBI task force
SPECIALITY: Stopping bad guys in their tracks
INTERESTS: His own career

G-FORCE UNDER THREAT

Talking animals are just a step too far for Killian and he is horrified to discover Ben has been working unsupervised. With his eye on the rule book, he orders Ben's lab to be closed down immediately!

DID YOU KNOW?
The FBI was founded in 1908 so it is over 100 years old. Its motto is "Fidelity, bravery, and integrity".

AGENT CARTER

Carter and his associate Trigstad provide back-up for Killian. Carter doesn't hold back his contempt for the G-Force and calls them gophers. Any fool can see they're guinea pigs! The G-Force are not impressed.

FACT FILE

NAME: Carter
ROLE: FBI agent
SPECIALITY: Sidekick to Killian
INTERESTS: Finding the perfect pair of shades

MEN IN BLACK

Trained to follow orders without question, these two guys, Carter and Trigstad, charge into situations with little thought. It makes them pretty easy to fool.

NEMESIS

Killian is tough, highly trained, and armed, but firepower won't work against this enemy. Something more ingenious is required – something more up the street of G-Force.

AGENT TRIGSTAD

Kitted out in sunglasses, dark suits, and standard-issue ear-pieces, Trigstad and his partner Carter mean business. Like Carter, Trigstad doesn't have much time for animals.

FACT FILE

NAME: Trigstad
ROLE: FBI agent
SPECIALITY: Sidekick to Killian
INTERESTS: Looking tough

PET SHOP

Elia's Pet Shop is where dreams come true! The friendly staff, Rosalita and Terrell, work tirelessly to bring pets together with families to love and care for them. With all the creature comforts you could want, the pet store is a comfortable place to live. But life only really has meaning for a pet when a little kid loves it with all their heart.

TERRELL
A dreamer, Terrell is a true animal lover. He is a little bit confused when he finds the G-Force in his truck!

ROSALITA
Señorita Rosalita is the cheery store manager. Always ready with a smile, she knows how to look after her customers.

HAMSTERS ARE PEOPLE TOO!
Don't be fooled by this cute furball! It's fair to say that Bucky has some issues and is quick to gloat at others' misfortune. He isn't pure hamster – his grandfather was a ferret (but don't tell anyone!) Aggressive Bucky is fiercely territorial. Beware crossing the line into his part of the cage!

DID YOU KNOW?

As well as hamsters and guinea pigs, Elia's has everything from mice and rabbits to lizards, snakes and iguanas!

SMILE!

It's not easy being chosen – 90 per cent of customers don't even make it past the puppies! Whenever someone ventures further into the shop, the competition is on between the animals to look as cute as possible. That's easier for some than others...

CURIOUS CUSTOMERS

Three guinea pigs and a mole turn up mysteriously in the shop. When first the FBI and then Ben and Marcie come asking for them, Rosalita is convinced something is going on!

ATTACK!

Just like pets, not all kids are adorable. One boy throws Hurley into the tarantula cage! The guinea pig narrowly escapes a spidery fate worse than death when Terrell rescues him.

HURLEY

Meet Hurley! He's a civilian, a typical guinea pig who's never met a secret agent before. Soft and squidgy, he has only ever known life in a pet store. Food falls from the sky, there's comfy bedding and no need to be house-trained. What more could a hamster want? The one thing missing is a family to love him. An eternal optimist, Hurley never gives up the dream of having somewhere to belong.

CAN WE SAVE THE WORLD — AFTER LUNCH?

WILD RIDE

When Hurley leaves the pet store, he gets more than he bargained for! But he steps up and proves that he can be a hero too.

THE TASTY LIFE

Roly-poly Hurley will eat anything, but his favourite is cake. Frosty chocolaty cake. He's heard a rumour about something called six-layer cake. Could it really exist?

FLUFFY

Squeezing through an air vent or doing push-ups may be tricky for soft-tummied Hurley, but he proves that size doesn't matter.

DID YOU KNOW?
Guinea pigs normally weigh 700–1200 g (1½–2½ lb) and are 20–25 cm (8–10 in) tall.

Hurley spends a lot of time thinking about his stomach.

Hurley hopes his cute quiff will help him get adopted.

AGENT HURLEY

The big wide world brings dangers but also the best prize of all: the G-Force becomes Hurley's family. He finally belongs and has an FBI Rookie badge to prove it!

FACT FILE

NAME: Hurley
SPECIALITY: Rookie
SKILLS: He's still working on it!
INTERESTS: Cake and cuddles

PET PEEVES

rapped in Elia's Pet Shop, the G-Force need a way out fast. Darwin masterminds a plan: they will look so adorable that they are adopted by a family. Once outside, they can then escape and all rendezvous at Ben's house. Sounds simple, huh? But none of the animals knows quite what is in store...

GRANDPA
Mr Goodman takes his grandkids, Penny and Connor, to Elia's Pet Shop to choose a pet. They leave with Juarez and Blaster – splitting up G-Force for the first time!

PENNY
Eight-year-old Penny has no time for moles like Speckles. She immediately chooses the beautiful Juarez.

THE GOODMANS' KITCHEN
The Goodmans' house is a typical family home – full of Saberling 5,000 appliances. The kitchen has a waste disposal... a toaster... a wafflemaker... it's like a Saber showroom!

LIVING DOLL

To Penny, Juarez is just like a living, breathing doll. She loves dressing her up like a princess in pretty pink gowns, bows, ribbons, nail polish and lipstick. Penny thinks she looks beautiful – Juarez couldn't disagree more!

CONNOR

Big brother Connor can be a little boisterous with his pets. Sensitive and fragile Hurley gets a narrow escape when Connor chooses to take Blaster home instead.

ESCAPE!

After Juarez and Blaster leave the store, Bucky reveals a trap door under his bedding. Darwin grabs the opportunity and scrambles. Once outside, he runs into a surprise – Hurley followed him out! (or rather, Bucky pushed him from the cage!) At first Darwin doesn't want responsibility for clueless Hurley, but the two soon become friends and Hurley proves to be a valuable asset to the G-Force.

SPEED JUNKIE

Connor isn't everyone's ideal owner, but he suits Blaster! The fearless guinea pig thrives on the speed and adrenalin of Connor's mini demolition derby. Blaster takes the joyriding one step further by using the car to escape with Juarez.

GO G-FORCE!

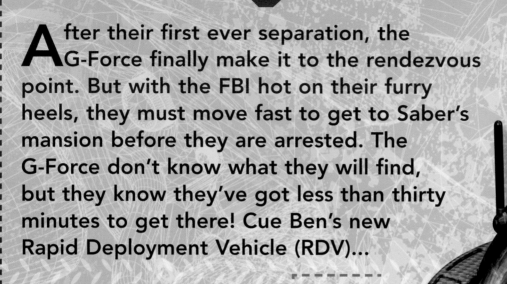

After their first ever separation, the G-Force finally make it to the rendezvous point. But with the FBI hot on their furry heels, they must move fast to get to Saber's mansion before they are arrested. The G-Force don't know what they will find, but they know they've got less than thirty minutes to get there! Cue Ben's new Rapid Deployment Vehicle (RDV)...

Machine can do 105 km (65 miles) an hour with the throttle wide open.

RDV: Rapid Deployment Vehicle

Juarez's ball is pink.

These are no ordinary hamster balls — they are driven by gyros with a steering wheel and levers.

BEN'S HOUSE

The rendezvous point, Ben's house, is constructed out of giant containers. Another great use of recycling materials!

SIZE IS EVERYTHING

The FBI's SUVs may be fast and look fierce, but the guinea pigs' rides have one key advantage – their small size means they can outmanoeuvre even the best FBI driver.

Air vents enable creatures to breathe in transit.

RDV can separate into three spheres – to divide and conquer!

HOLD TIGHT!

Travelling by RDV is a whole new experience for scaredy-cat Hurley – his stomach doesn't cope well with all the action-adventure!

Blaster drives the blue ball and Darwin the grey one.

Crazed hairdryer

Vicious blender

Evil coffeemaker

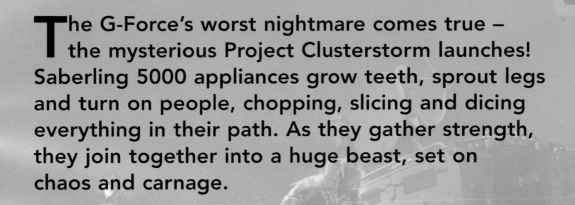

The G-Force's worst nightmare comes true — the mysterious Project Clusterstorm launches! Saberling 5000 appliances grow teeth, sprout legs and turn on people, chopping, slicing and dicing everything in their path. As they gather strength, they join together into a huge beast, set on chaos and carnage.

PEST CONTROL

Behind the evil plan is not Saber, but Speckles, one of the G-Force's own! Corrupted by grief and anger, he wanted revenge against humans. As Mr Yanshu, he fooled Saber and weaponised SaberSense. His plan is only foiled when Darwin loads an extermination virus into his computer system. Finding it hard to believe a friend betrayed them, Darwin offers Speckles a paw to save him, but he refuses and falls into the abyss.

DID YOU KNOW?
"Yanshu" — as in Mr Yanshu, Saber's shadowy associate — is the Chinese word for "Mole". The clue was right there all the time!

ALL NEW G-FORCE TEAM!

After the G-Force save the world from Speckles's crazed Project Clusterstorm, the FBI is forced to admit that G-Force rules! Ben gets funding for an official laboratory and the team are all given their own official FBI badges.

AGENT DARWIN
Riding high on the success of his mission, Darwin has overcome his self-doubt and is raring to lead his new team.

FBI
G-FORCE SPECIAL AGENT
DARWIN
FEDERAL BUREAU OF INVESTIGATION

AGENT BLASTER
Things won't be slowing down for Blaster. Far from it! But he still doesn't know where he stands with Juarez – girls are complicated!

FBI
G-FORCE SPECIAL AGENT
BLASTER
FEDERAL BUREAU OF INVESTIGATION

AGENT JUAREZ

Proud of her official FBI status, Juarez can't wait for the next mission. But it won't keep her too busy to carry on teasing Blaster!

FBI
G-FORCE
SPECIAL AGENT
JUAREZ
- - - - - - - - - - - - - - - - - - -
FEDERAL BUREAU OF INVESTIGATION

AGENT MOOCH

Fly-on-the wall Mooch will still be buzzing about on missions – if he can keep his eyes off sugary treats!

FBI
G-FORCE
SPECIAL AGENT
MOOCH
- - - - - - - - - - - - - - - - - - -
FEDERAL BUREAU OF INVESTIGATION

AGENT HURLEY

Fighting crime is a family business – and that includes Hurley too!

FBI
G-FORCE
ROOKIE
HURLEY
- - - - - - - - - - - - - - - - - - -
FEDERAL BUREAU OF INVESTIGATION

AGENT BUCKY?

The G-Force team is expanding and there's space for Bucky too. But whether or not he'll behave is another story...

G-FORCE

Disney

DK

LONDON, NEW YORK, MUNICH,
MELBOURNE, AND DELHI

Project Editor Elizabeth Dowsett
Project Art Editor Julie Thompson
Managing Editor Catherine Saunders
Publishing Manager Simon Beecroft
Art Director Lisa Lanzarini
Category Publisher Alex Allan
Production Controller Nick Seston
Production Editor Sean Daly

Written by Elizabeth Dowsett

First published in the Great Britain in 2009
by Dorling Kindersley Limited.
80 Strand, London, WC2R 0RL

Page design copyright © 2009 Dorling Kindersley Limited
A Penguin Company

2 4 6 8 10 9 8 7 6 5 4 3 2 1
GD137 – 04/09

Based on the screenplay by The Wibberleys and
Ted Elliott & Terry Rossio and Tim Firth
Based on a story by Hoyt Yeatman
Executive Producers Mike Stenson, Chad Oman,
Duncan Henderson, David James
Produced by Jerry Bruckheimer
Directed by Hoyt Yeatman

A CIP catalogue record for this book is available from the
British Library.

ISBN: 978-1-40534-114-1

Reproduced by Alta Image, London
UK edition printed and bound in Slovakia by TBB
Australian edition printed and bound in China by L-Rex

Discover more at
www.dk.com